How To Find All Missing Persons / Unsolved Cases. And Collect All Reward Offers. Volume XXXXVI. THE CASE OF JEVELLE BALMAIN-SMITH

DAVID GOMADZA

www.twofuture.world

How To Find All Missing Persons / Unsolved Cases. And Collect All Reward Offers. Volume XXXXVI. THE CASE OF JEVELLE BALMAIN-SMITH

Copyright © 2024 David Gomadza

All rights reserved.

Paperback ISBN: 9798329001990

How To Find All Missing Persons / Unsolved Cases. And Collect All Reward Offers. Volume XXXXVI. THE CASE OF JEVELLE BALMAIN-SMITH

DEDICATION

To a better future.

How To Find All Missing Persons / Unsolved Cases. And Collect All Reward Offers. Volume XXXXVI. THE CASE OF JEVELLE BALMAIN-SMITH

How To Find All Missing Persons / Unsolved Cases. And Collect All Reward Offers. Volume XXXXVI. THE CASE OF JEVELLE BALMAIN-SMITH

CONTENTS

How To Find All Missing Persons /
Unsolved Cases.
And Collect All Reward Offers. Volume XXXXVI.
THE CASE OF JEVELLE BALMAIN-SMITH 1
Afterlife Conversation.

and The Court Of Creation.   6

The Killers.   18

How To Find All Missing Persons / Unsolved Cases. And Collect All Reward Offers. Volume XXXXVI. THE CASE OF JEVELLE BALMAIN-SMITH

How To Find All Missing Persons / Unsolved Cases. And
Collect All Reward Offers. Volume XXXXVI. THE CASE OF JEVELLE
BALMAIN-SMITH

ACKNOWLEDGMENTS

Tomorrow's World Order

How To Find All Missing Persons / Unsolved Cases. And Collect All Reward Offers. Volume XXXXVI. THE CASE OF JEVELLE BALMAIN-SMITH

How To Find All Missing Persons / Unsolved Cases. And Reward Offers. Volume XXXXVI. THE CASE OF JEVELLE BALMAIN-SMITH

BACKGROUND INFORMATION

The NSW Government, together with the NSW Police Force, has announced a $1 million reward for information into the disappearance of Revelle Balmain more than 26 years ago

Revelle Balmain, then aged 22, was last seen in the Kingsford area on Saturday 5 November 1994.

Her personal property – including a make-up bag, keys and a shoe – was later found scattered near Ainslie Street.

Ms Balmain was reported missing later that evening and has not been seen or heard from since

disappearance has caused immeasurable grief to her family for more than 26 years.

"For many years, our family worked tirelessly to find out what happened to my sister – but sadly both our mother and Revelle's father, Ivor, passed away without ever knowing what happened to their little girl," Ms Simpson said.

"Losing someone that is close to you – you're never the same person again. I truly hope this reward will prompt someone to come forward with information that will help police find those responsible for Revelle's disappearance.

"It is my personal hope that this reward may also help us find Revelle – so that I may finally put her to rest," Ms Simpson said.

Anyone with information that may assist Strike Force Aramac detectives is urged to contact Crime Stoppers: 1800 333 000 or https://nsw.crimestoppers.com.au. Information is treated in strict confidence. The public is reminded not to report information via NSW Police social media pages.

Click here for more information on Revelle Balmain on the NSW Police Force Missing Persons Enquiry System.

https://www.police.nsw.gov.au/can_you_help_us/rewards/1000000_reward/20080730_reward_to_solve_disappearance_and_murder_of_revelle_balmain

How To Find All Missing Persons / Unsolved Cases. And Collect All Reward Offers. Volume XXXXVI. THE CASE OF JEVELLE BALMAIN-SMITH

TOMORROW'S WORLD ORDER'S PERSPECTIVES

USE OF PREDEFINED AFTERLIFE PARAMETERS

These guide souls the moment it exist the human body on its journey to Yahweh the creator these define what to do and what to expect as you go to hell or heaven if a souk leaves earth it enters ozone orbit and instantly everything reboots for it to start a new phase of life after living the earth's body now what happens is that it enters the ozone orbit and a simply click caused by the sudden drop of pressure from -1186 to – 20 means the bottom shaft of the soul will lift rapidly and this pushes its back into the air higher than its head best example is a penguin but with real human legs and head just the shape now God created a life predefined program for them instead of asking what should I do and where should I go they instantly know from predefined stencils if you did well and talked most about God then heaven is for you if you did evil and talked more about the devil then the devil is yours now if we Ask what can be of humans without souks this is the answer dead forever your soul is you a new transformation to the electromagnetic waves life where you see Yahweh for the first time and praise him and wish you had seen him a long time ago because of his Majesty and will always be there forever now what are all these you may ask these are rules to be guided by in the creation court in short it has everything humans know about the judges and the presiding judge who will always be Yahweh and 84 angels surrounding the altar 28 high priests who always say Yahweh have mercy on humans and 74 smaller courts priests who always say Yahweh has mercy on humans and 96 princesses who say glory to Yahweh forever and ever amen we have 96 elders who always say if I can why he can't meaning if the devil can drink blood why can't Yahweh who created the devil and blood do the same now this is not the same as saying if the devil can kill why can Yahweh its more on professional grounds rather than challenging now if we look at the inside of the court we have 81 priests surrounding the altar who say Yahweh be merciful to humans but if they disobey you we put hem on trial for you and kill them for you almighty Yahweh inside this is a round circle where Yahweh sits and asks questions now if we look deep inside the court you will see that there are other things that resemble earth high courts like benches and chairs 10 times human sizes for the gods who are so enormous 2 are equal to 84 billion humans in size

predefined parameters for humans after death as in know what is inside is a large size of books the book of creation is among them with 1089786789283678901234867890124586178901 pages and is divided into humans first then chapter for animals then a chapter for angles then a chapter for gods and a chapter for Joseph Yahweh's best friend and a chapter for Yahweh's best friend's wife Anna and a chapter for Yahweh's wife Catitighit and lastly a chapter for Yahweh and recently a chapter for davidgomadza as Yahweh's representative on earth marking the new beginnings starting in 2025

1. tell us who killed you
2. tell us what killed you
3. tell us why and who killed you
4. tell us why you died
5. tell us what could have been done and is not done
6. tell us what could be and why
7. tell is when this happened
8. tell us why this is so
9. tell us why this is so
10. what can be done to improve this

What does the book of creation say about davidgomadza David Gomadza is the first and last ruler to be appointed by Yahweh fir the next 25 billion years and will act as his representative on earth deciding cases and upholding his principles on earth and as such has been entitled to 489 trillion dollars in assets this number signifies eternity among humans and the beginning of a new Era chapter 78678928028938628418902876890183208678901234867890182364 87289128610 Creation manual the new Era of new electromagnetic wave conduit signed and dated by Yahweh himself on 27may2024 at 237800 Yatime
creation.universe.ya.start.end.find.davidgomadza.ya.askya.ya

Ask.read.creation.manucreation.universe.ya.start.end.find.davidgoma askya.ya

Ask.rulesofthecourt.start.now.start
David Gomadza welcome the rules of court are guiding principles that tell you what to do and how to do it first you must always say I believe in the court of creation and I shall abide by he rules of this court and shall always do things according to the rules of this court in deciding the cases I am assigned to you must ask what can be done so that you know all your options before making choices the court system will make it easy to check files and ask the outcomes of the decision ask the court the final decision in any case.

THE AFTERLIFE CONVERSATION AND THE COUNCIL OF CREATION'S ANAYLSIS.

jevelle balmain
god i died today the 18th of october 1974 at aseropts aerosp's house after i came looking for a one time squank sex to use when i get married tomorrow 19 of october 1974 i am supposed first to change my name back to jevelle balmain-smith from the current jevelle balmain this is because as i just found out at the reception that the police especially pc aerost aeropmn deliberately swapped our houses with another lady possibly the one i saw in the fridge at the giants house one without a vagina now this is my story i woke up early in the morning and said i am rich tomorrow on my birthday i am going to get married very early i waited for sex this is my first time with a man and heard it hearts so i am tensing all the time but when i saw him in person he look like a half wit and violence is within him i made myself feel at home then i realised that he had a strange smell i never smelled before but so familiar i swear i smelled this before when my dad died in the house person smell different and i went for a check and toy shock but not surprise i found another woman with real knickers dirty as well with sperm warm in the fridge that means when i came i disturbed him screwing a dead corpse but what scared me the most is that she was chewed between the legs blood was there

it look like she had a tight vagina and he had to remove the piece to fit a never had sex that freaked me out if he can do this then what about a virgin she looked old with a sagging face but blond so i said i am going i will come back some time then he said okay then let me open the door but he listened to something and said no wait we go together h8and i agreed then he grabbed my neck and said we can fuck today please don't say no because that would hurt and said okay we can so what we do first we must eat and i don't want you to eat me as a joke then he stopped and said what i said that's a joke and he said did you see something at the house i said no just a joke to make you relax so we have great sex and then he said i have food
pc aterop ares said to him we want both these ladies dead i am telling you as your boss not as a policemen today we need to get rid of these cheeky ladies forever okay so this is what you do ask to wait for me if she runs away then leave her she will have given you the respect you deserve but if not then grab her neck and fill your dick inside her cummings inside her that feeling you would kill for right because i would kill for to you to be eaten by you after great sex i would love that so can we come when you are having a great time or you have a great time first then we come after to kill you and send you to them as r that now just imagine the best virgin in town coming well because you too now know too much so we might as well kill you just imagine someone knowing that surely he will break lose the whole police force will be destroyed that we pray on the weak but rich for their property this is true because i want janine's house for 20 dollars and pc aers want jevelle's house so we teamed up and make sure that we kill all today and swap their houses then send the documents to the police housing association and then take the houses for ourselves then sell all in 5 years for 2 million that's being clever so if we can we can do this now or wait when we are 60 to enjoy more money in the police where rewards top up our millionaire accounts for the next 100 years without a single human being able to solve any case but only god even if he did we can actually hide his evidence or swap it around unless he is to publish as books that he can use later to prove we steal without this then we are safe but then again where us god people were looking for god for years above all we can divert that send.ya to ourselves now using a simple code

08923678902867890289038678901 8 that means that yahweh will always be there but we are now the people's god the reason why the force is doing this is to be able to stand the pressure for change and returning of these houses since 1948 as i understand this is the year this began in europe due to the 1948 convention of human rights that took away powers used by the queen to take property from orphans who would eventually lose the property through an underground operation termed then capital gains tax verdict act that was hidden but operated everywhere the first reason police took part in this scam is that they believed they gain as well free house for 20 and 1 million guaranteed at age 60 of retirement through the use of other accounts to receive money the accounts are synchronized to real accounts through a chip system that says ask.ya.620 this send all your funds to one place and you wi get a notification when done that says you received cash from a source this source is the consolidation system of the police who send money to hide accounts once that is done then this credited to your accounts the next day in real times when you check your accounts then you will see real money in this is why most people believe because the money comes to your account without a trace so this means this works now if i ask what can a this mean for the future this means that we can solve all our problems in the future so the job is secure than the current system statistics that say that this is wrong now if we ask what else can this mean for others that means we are crooks growing at the expense of others especially the women and children who are exploited by others who took oath to protect now it's you stealing and killing all these by commands if we look at these two cases i think the women didn't have to die but could have been squanked and left to start their ives as millionaires but these people had other ideas and had death and property in mind something now called dap in mind meaning to gain property you must cause death this is now common but is wrong what can be done

1. we can enforce this and prevent stealing of property of orphans bu securing their rights through double proofing where the bank must add another signature before the police can take the property as theirs which is happening even now even today a woman lost property to the police in 2024 this is wrong her name is eunice herstert from

canada

2. we can look at this law and establish a law that prevents the taking of these properties by the police
3. we can educate people and make them aware of our work and help others work hard as we and not look to cheap deals the police have become the robbers this is said
then he started asking about the house and why the police want the house and i said they are cheating people and collecting capital gains tax that is not even due what if i don't sale then what i can say that they have become greedy and literary taking the house of victims even before they know what they have done if this is not the case then they are involved because by law they must find out the reasons why this is happening a woman missing from last week that janine they too her house today it's in the papers because they are saying that if she don't come back the bank will take the house and the police must protect the capital gains tax this is wrong because we are getting killed for nothing then i realised what i said okay today we can even fuck because they are calling for me to check the property and he said just te me who and i will kill him tomorrow and eat him and did not laugh but cried and said that's why my mum said iust be strong or else i will lose the house to these crooks so i said so why do you kill her the woman in the fridge and this was my mistake otherwise i had worn but he stood up and ran yo check as if he had forgotten and came back and said left fuck before you run and tell the police and said i see what they are doing send you to check on me i askyself what the richest women see in me both with houses and no men i thought it's all because of the pice stressing you now you want a real man but now you run to them makes sense because they will steal your house anywhere better if you let them that way you have yourife they will never ask me to kill you then she stood up and ran to the door and opened it and left sprinting but the squanks had started and the panic sends huge cramps to the legs and she couldn't escape he laughed when he saw her in one place unable to move and said today is my luck day thank you god because this woman would have got me shot by these crooks stealing orphans"s houses and he grabbed her and made her open the door by her head as advised by

pc aerops who said let her open the door by her head you said she can but i think she can't and they switched the cops using a code 087654321098678920 that switched what he heard to what he thoughts so that it looks like he argued that she can open the door with her head but he meant using brain thoughts i stanly he said open the closed door and pushed her so hard against the door that her naked broke literally that she could not lift it and from that moment she bent down that he got aroused and opened the door and started having sex with her until her spirit ran out and stopped and looked at him to identify him through facial features then he said where are you going so fast as if you are late for something and it said literally i died so why i stay on earth i must go to heaven i heard hell reception and he said i don't believe such a beautiful well behaved woman go to hell what about me who kill then it said he is asking where he goes and instantly an answer came that said heaven with god so it flew so fast to offset that record by flying the fastest time recorded in the history of creation when it reached hell reception it was only 8 seconds the journey that take 8 minutes from earth to heaven at the reception they told her to wait for Yahweh but he never came the reason is because Yahweh don't normally see people who die having sex.

i am revelle balmain i was killed by a man called aerops atere and he said what can be of prostitute with no money to pay but i said i don't prostitute and if i did then none of your business then he said okay i will make it mine and he grabbed me by the neck and bent me down and tried to remove my knickers but i killed him hard then i ran but he followed and said i fucken kill you today if i have to come back and give me or you are dead meat so i ran as fast as i can but somehow i could not pace out as much so he stabled but he caught me and dragged me back to his house and pushed me hard to break my neck that my head never stood still again i heard creatures talking inside me one said long ago 8 minutes then changed to 2 minutes and he went to get a big knife and threw it at me and i died
long ago statistics
as0 20
as13 8

as6 10
as7 8
as7 9
as2 7
as6 8
as9 10
as16 8
as7 13
as4 7
as3 10
as2 1
as7 9
as6 17
as20 21
as22 80
as23 10
as24 6
as25 8
as26 9
as28 10
as32 8
as33 99
as44 78
as29 3

now if we look at these statistics you can see that she died of lack of oxygen in the head that's why after she can hear or talk to fix is to add oxygen from atmosphere at rebirth

the court ruled that she was killed by aserops ators who said if i can then you can but then touched his penis and rubbed his hands but she said no i am not a prostitute so fuck off then he chased and broke her neck causing an early death in which Yahweh gave her a code 8267890284867890284867890023489018 to take with during rebirth her current coordinates are
8978678902834567890282789028367890028456789028410
or
28.28678902
29.3867854321

in a marked grave at a cemetery on top of someone else who is named as asetopq meaning asover aertp who is in the grave below her her death has been marked as the worst recorded in history she suffocated to death in 2 seconds instead of 8 seconds which was initially given then she ran out of oxygen then died but her soul made it to heaven where Yahweh promised her rebirth but ever since she had been waiting but is healed though

my name is aterops ateret i work hard at work as a train driver and lately i have been feeling to kill myself but i found peace i was so obsessed with sex that if i don't get i feel like killing women especially those who refuse and i asked one for sex i said nicely what can i do for you for sex and she mocked me and said i can but only if i was so fuck you and that really hurts so i grabbed her by the head and sent her knocking the door with her head if i ask nicely no one listen but like this i get the respect i deserve so before she died i said she if you had agreed it could all be finished by now and she lifted her middle finger and died so i laughed and said i will fuck continuously for the next 40 years and kill as well if these bitches don't want to open legs when i want to

pc aoper said of him if only man were born to fuck then he would collect a price and he labeled fucker of the century but then he had his own problems like erectile dysfunction then he asked a boy then a woman now teenagers now he just put it anywhere he pleases last time it was that girl that disappeared the next day and now it's jevelle balmain i think he killed her and hide her in a pit but we must ask for him so we know where he is putting all these bodies before it's toolate

pc astnop said he will let all those around him feel uneasy with the way he demands sex from everyone now what next rape everyone or even kill all those who refuse

jevelle balmain

i can ran from this monster and enjoy the rest of the day why did i come to his house in the first place and she said i wish i had stayed home maybe he won't let me go after seeing another dead women in the fridge now he will just kill me without any bargain if i can tell the police then he can still kill me now what can i do to be safe and he looked at me as if i saw that body but that time i had not i came

for sex last time he was so good i literally squirt in his face and he said i can if you can then we both laughed but this time the house smell strange meat so i went to check the fridge there is a woman a real person blond with one eye missing and vagina removed but maybe it's not real but the first sight is so awful i nearly threw up
i died 2 days ago my name is janine vaughan i was killed by aserops ateret sometimes he say atere but he strangled me then ate my eye and said it's delicious before i died then died and when i died as my brain tells me he cut out my vagina and said i can if you can then he screamed as something got into his eye then came back and said human eyes talk so i laughed even if i were dead then he said if i can you can but i am dead then i realised that he had been with another girl who opened the fridge and screamed then closed and walked out slowly then grabbed her and they fucked then i realised that i was not dead long ago started when he pushed my vagina all in then held my neck and squeezed as if he was doing my neck saying go there and hold the tightest go now before i kill her the more you delay the more she dies then i passed out then i screamed so loud that if there were neighbour's then he would have been caught in the act now he is planning to bury everything and pretend this never happened now if i ask he said i have another ask dot what about me and i get this i have another bye you die now okay look your vagina is gone now then what who want arse i kill anyone who say arse then he mastered what is needed to make a woman gloat because realizing that i had no vagina made me want to kill him but then the people would think i am a lunatic but i don't care i might be dead by now but look now i am still alive but long ago has started again 2seconds left then i died this time i went to hell reception decorated with flowers and marine wild it looked so cute that i said who did these and they said the black servants and i said there are black servants and the angel said yes but they only wake when everyone is asleep
i opened the fridge and the head moved and i touched it real human head so today i will say i don't want sex and run because after sex he is going to kill me when i sat down i spread my legs so he see vagina and go and master bate as he does then come for his long one that i squirt as well but he looked and come straight to me and today upset he is shaking but someone talks to him today he said she saw and

silent then if she can then i can then stopped as the words played in my mouth and he continued he said if
i am pc atopser i work with people to keep our interest high regarding the project we call aert because we must make sure that we get rid of all these orphans who own houses as per the queen elizabeth charter of 1665 according to the records i am looking at recorded in england on the 11 day of june 1665 marked as official secret where the queen must shade the blood of orphans and take their houses and give them to his locals who are us and the soldiers but never heard of the soldiers if i can then he will i sent all these women to him for sex and he murder and bury all in the cemetery according to the plan we laid out where each individual person is arranged to correspond to their opposite in alphabetical order where one way is the reverse of the other for example in this case we are witnessing janine vaughan is the opposite of jevelle balmain in that jv is the same as jb if we look at backward and forward if we start where we start from a then v is the same as b as v is the second later after b in the senoiet alphabet which we will use for all cases forever where

a is o
b is z
c is j
d is o
e is j
f is n
g is k
h is e
i is z
j is s
k is d
l is t
m is n
n is p
o is a
p is r
q is h
r is u

s is y
t is l
u is v
v is b
w is z
now if we say jon doe this means fap oaj
that means if we want to know what account is being given money this time we need to check and convert to our secret language and alphabetic order so if you see a name like asert this means in real life ojhpl now ask what is asert then it will say asert is ojhpl now take this ojhpl and put it back in reverse order to find the true meaning this means
l for t
p for n
h for q
j for7 e
o for a
that means the account is that of aeqnt
that's how we trace accounts to individual s
if i ask these women for sex it's like a taboo something that can't be done and as such something that cause death but in actual fact refusing is potentially something that cause death because if i can't get then i am just going to kill because the cops want these women's houses so they collect capital gains tax they actually told me what to do as a secret but i can say that they are recruiting officers easily because they promise them money from rewards of these women i refused because how can a prostitute generate income he said we generate but what i refused is that all the money goes to those who were already gifted there meaning free while others have to work for it there's get 100000 for free they create a drill then use the drill to gather money then use this money to fund other drills this way all the drills are potentially of generating enough cash to make even more money this is how this works one deposits money into one account then the other deposit in all accounts then another meaning spreading the money so that in the end they will have more money all not sure how those at the top make it but it's along those lines he then sat down and picked up revellee who he had just broke her neck

and touched her vagina and said still hot man i could had enjoyed it while it was great but never mind i have food and sex and he laughed then removed all her clothes and had sex with her then the next day took both the women for burial according to pc asert he was supposed to bury all in the cemetery bit in order the person with the name that start a must be last and the person with a word that start with z must be first then as per above alphabetic order convert so that if its j then this is s and so on

after killing them i carried them one by one to the grave i carried first janine who i had killed then she said bruuuhh then i dropped her and laughed i saw big hole and threw her in there then went back to collect jevelle balmain who was still fresh so i did her 10 times then threw her in the same pit then collected woods and timber and covered the top and went back and guess who was there waiting for me pc aserops who said we heard screams who and where then i said your mother in your arse go before i kill this shit then fuck it then he said okay i will go if that how you think of and he left but returned with another and said if i can then what can be of him and shot me in the stomach i rolled down and my aty said 8 seconds long ago then an animal screamed and said we are going to lose him check ast and as9 then calculate heart rate then i can check everything else he then started shaking violently and said what can be of officers who get women killed for capital gains tax he said they will rot in hell

the coordinates for all 08983867890284678902678902867892841892838768928378910672486789210 at asert cemetery all in a grave marked as eterty at the entrance to the graveyard and the tombstone is marked as if yes then let's start now but if no then who cares human coordinates are of the same place 29.38726836

27.2829367890

at the junction of 87 north of pensualvenia usa

near the city of asert

geolocation coordinates are 87.2787923810

80.78284867890218

marked as if you can but why can't you in white chalk at the corner the end.

janine vaughan

lord i come to you today i was killed by aerops aerotp who said what can i do for you for sex and i said as if i am a prostitute then he said it's helping each other as humans and he said yes better help others than be dead look this dick need vagina all the time so are you going to help or die your choice today i don't let anyone decide i decide tired of everyone deciding for themselves no one decide for me and always starve me so today either you do what i want or die it's not rocket science today i decide then i wanted to give in because i was afraid now at his yard in person he is so scary than what they portray on pictures i wanted great big dick sex so i said i want to find the biggest once before i get married and ride it hard so that if i meet a small guy with everything small i can use this as hold all married women do this others no would marry anyone they are with so i was given a tip that we have one in the city then i thought why not pay him i own a house fully paid i just pay bills of what we use and i save 800 dollars after collecting rent and paying everything after my father left the house and money for me then died then i had no idea i just turned 18 yesterday and i have a house to collect and today i enjoy great sex tomorrow i enjoy great money but the problem is the police especially pc astero mnopqrstuvw meaning stuort who keep coming and asking if i paid capital gains but i say no only after selling do you have to pay these capital gains taxes otherwise don't even bother coming i fed up seeing ugly faces all the time when i have a house worth 2million dollars if i have to sell it tomorrow so go fuck mama's pu go little hebo in australian local means cow boy with shit in the arse and he said i am so mean but i said you have no right to ask me about capital gains taxes today you wait until the house is sold then ask otherwise i put a complaint for harassment you come back her smiling like a big i fins someone to pay and fuck your brains with a stone okay now go shit hay and he walked but stopped i am pc asterot aserop i am concerned about women in this neighborhood who work up and found out that they own a house worth 2 million dollars but without any income at all if they lose that house its capital gains lost hence we must make sure we know what is going on i went to see two women today janine vaughan and jevelle balmain who are all house owners but literally dick heads both are after squank fucks with the most dangerous beast in town asertop aserop who as i know made 3 women disappear on the same day without a trace i have been to his place and he threaten to kill fuck and cook me and that is a hellraiser itself cooking is okay but fucking another man is wrong but i think starvation can lead him along that road today this janine was so mean she called me names that it hurts to think that daddy's girl has grown up and start following the road papa took of scolding at the hard working police and said you tart boy don't come here again okay or someone will fuck your brains with a brick why don't you listen and know that capital gains taxes are collected at the end instead of at the beginning but that's where i think she is wrong if we wait after she lost the property what good is there for us put yourself in my shoes this is the case of we let her screw giants with no job all money will go to giant but who will pay she is refusing help what i am teaching her is that accept anyone at your property as long as the property is full you have money but she rents 6 out of 10 rooms and choose who to rent to all the time at least 4 are empty i said even if i am trash then as long as i pay bills then that's okay but today i had no business going there then i got what i deserved but i think she had no idea what the giant can do i swear the giant is the one killing people only that i don't know what happens behind the scene but where he hides the bodies is anyone's guess since he started working at the cemetery a lot of graves have been dug up and refill again if you ask him why this is his reply i can so why you ask maybe you want to top someone else otherwise mind your fucking business first day i got upset and said i get you arrested and he lived and said try now and see who gets eaten so i thought it's a joke and he nearly crack opened my skull i had no business being there so i took 8 months off work to heal and had operation to hide the wound this is giant and i see these horny loaded women all going there maybe asking for marriage to find someone to protect the house that can't do that will mean for 2 years we have tailed them we got nothing a waste of time so to prevent all this and payback i devised a plan that both women perish at the same time and are buried in the same grave and at the same time so that when it comes to identify them then there are complications where the house of one is given to the wrong one that way when we take them for free and give them to the housing council then there won't be problems the problems comes when you can assign a house to a person so we can't take janine vaughan house and give it to jevelle balmain but we can take both and give them to the police housing association as unidentified and for disposal and not keeping but if we keep then we have to get avidaffits from the court we promised 25% of the value at sell that means that no one will refuse so its a win win situation now what i was saying is that after some time then we can tell who the house was but geolocating them we can say geolocate janine all the time and our computer typology will show us her coordinates all the time then we do the same with jevelle and get the coordinates then decide but this is not a big issue the issue is how do we make the women disappear we can easily let giant dump both in a pit grave or just bury them on top of another called topping secretly so we spend years looking for them

YOU MUST READ ALSO THE CASE OF JANINE VAUGHAN

THE KILLERS THE CONFESSIONS AND THE COORDINATES

aseropts aerosp's also known as aerops atere and he said what can be of prostitute with no money to pay but i said i don't prostitute and if i did then none of your business then he said okay i will make it mine and he grabbed me by the neck who
The house papers were mixed then lost and the police had to get the papers to match janini to her house jevelle to hers and later took all the houses and sold all for 2million each and asked a policem to distribute the proceeds to 21 accounts each topping up with 200000 per account

the whole police force will be destroyed that we pray on the weak but rich for their property this is true because i want janine's house for 20 dollars and pc aers want jevelle's house so we teamed up and make sure that we kill all today and swap their houses then send the documents to the police housing association and then take the houses for ourselves then sell all in 5 years for 2 million that's being clever so if we can we can do this now or wait when we are 60 to enjoy more money in the police where rewards top up our millionaire accounts for the next 100 years

…I found God…visit www.twofuture.world

How To Find All Missing Persons / Unsolved Cases. And Collect All Reward Offers. Volume XXXXVI. THE CASE OF JEVELLE BALMAIN-SMITH

THE CLAIM

the reward offer

THE COLLECTION

www.twofuture.world/donate

ABOUT DAVID GOMADZA

visit www.twofuture.world

signed david gomadza
ask.davidgomadzaauthorised.licensed.checkya.askya.ya

19 June 2024 22.29 pm
scotland
00447719210295
davidgomadza@hotmail.com
info@twofuture.world

www.ingramcontent.com/pod-product-compliance
Lightning Source LLC
Chambersburg PA
CBHW031517210526
45464CB00007B/2945